SEE A PLANT GROW!

APPLE

by Charlie W. Sterling

TABLE OF CONTENTS

tadpole books

WORDS TO KNOW

apples

flowers

leaves

roots

seed

stem

APPLE

We plant a seed.

roots

It grows roots.

It grows a stem.

It grows leaves.

It grows into a tree.

It grows flowers.

It grows apples!

LET'S REVIEW!

Apples start as seeds. They grow into fruit. What colors are the apples below?

INDEX